Bradwell's ECLECTICA LIVERPOOL

Published by Bradwell Books
9 Orgreave Close Sheffield S13 9NP
Email: books@bradwellbooks.co.uk

© Rachel Atkinson-James 2014

The right of Rachel Atkinson-James as author of this work has been asserted by her in accordance with the Copyright, Design and Patents Act, 1988. All rights reserved. No part of this publication may be reproduced, stored in a retrieval system or transmitted in any form or by any means, electronic, mechanical, photocopying, recording or otherwise without the prior permission of Bradwell Books.

British Library Cataloguing in Publication Data: a catalogue record for this book is available from the British Library.

1st Edition

ISBN: 9781909914209

Print: Gutenberg Press, Malta

Design and artwork by: Andrew Caffrey

Photograph Credits:
Shutterstock, Getty Images, Andy/Susan Caffrey and Creative Commons (credited where known)

Bibliography

Liverpool: A People's History by PETER AUGHTON (Carnegie, 1990)

Scouse English by FRED FAZAKERLEY (Abson, 2001)

The Making of Liverpool by MIKE FLETCHER (Wharncliffe Books, 2004)

Made Up wi' Liverpool! by RON FREETHY (Countryside, 2007)

Talk like the Scousers by PETER GRANT (Trinity Mirror, 2008)

The Liverpool Book of Days by STEPHEN HORTON (History Press, 2012)

The Story of Liverpool by ALEXANDER TULLOCH (History Press, 2008)

http://www.freewebs.com/englishdialects/

http://www.bbc.co.uk/liverpool/localhistory/

http://liverpoolmurders.blogspot.co.uk/

http://liverpool-noise.co.uk/2013/11/16/project-scouse-food-liverpool/

http://www.liverpoolecho.co.uk/

http://www.paranormaldatabase.com/hotspots/liverpool.php

http://www.old-liverpool.co.uk/

http://www.wirralhistory.net/scouse1.html

http://liverpolitan.im/main/index.htm

Acknowledgements:

Thank you as always to all at Bradwell Books, but especially Chris Gilbert for advice, guidance and the occasional kick in the pants. Jonnie Robinson from the British Library was generous with time and advice regarding the Scouse dialect, and Andrew and Susan Caffrey made trips to Liverpool to research and photograph walks when I was unable to. My thanks to all of you.

Bradwell's ECLECTICA LIVERPOOL

Rachel Atkinson-James

BRADWELL BOOKS

Contents

6 INTRODUCTION
Founded by King John in 1207, Liverpool has always been a port city famous for the swagger, the sense of humour and the artistic creativity of its inhabitants.

15 HUMOUR
Direct, personal, often biting but never malicious, the Scouse sense of humour is famous the world over.

25 MURDERS
With gang-related street violence, the bodies of illegitimate children kept in boxes, arsenic poisonings and cinema shootings, Liverpool has seen no shortage of unsavoury goings-on.

9 LOCAL DIALECT
The Scouse dialect is a heady mix of Lancashire, Cheshire, Welsh and immigrant Irish. It exploded into the national consciousness in the 1960s and continues to evolve today.

19 RECIPES
Make a meal of Scouse, Liverpool's 'national dish', followed by a serving of Wet Nelly or a slice of Liverpool Tart.

33 LOCAL NAMES
The Stanley and Molyneux families were early rivals for power in the city, and their homes and names remain important in the local area.

WALKS
Two short walks, one around the town centre visiting Liverpool's most spectacular buildings and the other taking in the Albert Dock area with its famous 'Three Graces'.

LOCAL CUSTOMS
The footballing anthem *You'll Never Walk Alone* rings out from the Kop, and generations of Chinese and Irish immigrants bring their traditions to this cosmopolitan city.

LOCAL HISTORY
The city of Liverpool has always looked to the sea, with its history of maritime trade and immigration influencing its architecture, its transport and even its art and culture.

GHOST STORIES
Ghostly hitchhikers, mad wives, phantom chambermaids and the ghost of the first casualty of the railway network all haunt Liverpool's streets and buildings.

LOCAL SPORTS
Liverpudlians are passionate about sport, from the spectacle of the Grand National to footballing rivalries and even an early version of the Olympics!

FAMOUS LOCALS
Liverpool has produced famous and successful people across all walks of life, from astronomy, philanthropy and politics to the arts and showbusiness.

AUTHOR'S FOREWORD

As a very young child, I lived on Merseyside. My family moved there when I was a young baby, following my father's job, and my younger sister was born there. We lived in a flat in Bidston, a suburb of Birkenhead, and although we did not stay long (we left when I was not much more than three), family lore reports that our time there was happy. I must have made regular crossings to Liverpool on the Mersey ferry with my mother, although my hazy memories are limited to the dog that lived in the next-door flat (a black Labrador called Liesl) and an unrelated accident with a ladder.

Growing up in East Anglia, my Merseyside-born sister supported Liverpool FC with a passion, and we never forgot our connections with the north-west. Indeed, a part of our family history probably remains there – my mother lost her engagement ring while on a shopping trip in Liverpool city centre.

So – if anyone found an engagement ring in Liverpool some time around 1972, do please get in touch. Researching and writing this book has been an education, an inspiration and a labour of love, and I hope to have done some justice to the city which my family once called home.

Rachel Atkinson-James

INTRODUCTION

THE CITY OF LIVERPOOL WAS FOUNDED IN 1207 AS THE DIRECT RESULT OF KING JOHN'S EXPANSIONIST POLICY TOWARDS THE IRISH.

He found himself in need of a suitable port from which to embark his navy for a seaborne expedition to Ireland, so he sent his surveyors north and west in search of a suitable location. While scouring the coast of Cheshire and Lancashire they came across a tidal inlet in the estuary of the River Mersey, known locally as the Laver Pool for its deep slow-moving weed-choked water (laver is a kind of seaweed). They sent word to the King that a suitable embarkation point had been found.

SHUTTERSTOCK/ANT CLAUSEN

King John responded by creating a new Royal Borough named for the pool, and offering parcels of land (or burgages) in the new borough for sale to London merchants and nobles. Uptake was swift among interested parties from Lancashire and Cheshire as well as London, and the tiny marshland settlement of Liverpool grew rapidly to become a major port city.

Of course, the irony is that King John's original intention, to occupy Ireland and quell the troublesome natives, was rather subverted by the fact that Liverpool became one of the major immigration points to the UK, with many thousands of Irish settlers arriving in search of work or as a staging post on the way to the US. Much of the city's vibrancy comes from its eclectic mix of inhabitants, with Scots, Welsh and Irish settlers mixing with the Lancastrian locals and also with immigrants from much further afield. The city welcomed them all, and continues to do so.

The River Mersey remains the city's major artery, with the Port of Liverpool providing berths for trade, passenger and leisure vessels and the river linking to the rail and canal networks for onward inland travel. Down the centuries the city has traded in coal, wool, Sheffield steel, leather, cotton, tobacco, sugar and people, although its part in the reprehensible slave trade was more limited than is often believed.

From its inception the city and its inhabitants have enjoyed a reputation for a certain bolshiness, a swagger and sense of adventure that are reflected in Liverpool's history and its humour. Liverpudlians (or sometimes Liverpolitans) are known for their brashness and bluntness, their take-no-prisoners humour and their quick repartee, all underpinned by a passionate loyalty to their city, their family and friends. Scousers, the affectionate name most commonly given to residents of the city, comes from Scouse (or Lobscouse), the ubiquitous dish cooked and eaten by the poor and the itinerant maritime population. It consisted of a vegetable broth cooked up with whatever meat was available, often the poorest cuts (tripe, trotters, pigs' ears) and eked out to last the family as long as possible. These days the dish is cooked with better cuts of meat and is regarded as a local delicacy; there is even a vegetarian version!

The city went through a period of being renowned for all manner of social ills – there were ghettos of poverty, crime and the lowest standards of living, despite the city's enormous mercantile affluence in other areas. During the Victorian years it was known as the Black Spot on the Mersey, but at the same time it was also a powerhouse of industrial invention, witnessing the birth of the railways and the invention of many maritime and dockland innovations such as the complicated system of dry and wet docks. In recent years the city has undergone a renaissance and seen a huge amount of inward investment, with large swathes of previously unlovely industrial and dockland areas being redeveloped.

The middle of the twentieth century was a period of huge cultural and artistic expansion, with music and art exploding from Liverpool and conquering the world; this vibrancy has continued into the twenty-first century, and in 2008 the city was named the European City of Culture. Of course, music is part of Liverpool's artistic soul; the city is home to the UK's oldest professional symphony orchestra, the Royal Liverpool Philharmonic, and the Beatles led the Merseyside pop music revolution that conquered the world. Artists from Liverpool have included George Stubbs (famous for his pictures of horses), Brian Shields or Braaq (who painted northern industrial landscapes) and Bill Tidy, the well-known cartoonist. There is also a proud tradition of writers and dramatists, from Beryl Bainbridge and Clive Barker to Alan Bleasdale and Carla Lane, who have contributed to making the Scouse dialect one of the best known and most often imitated in the UK.

SHUTTERSTOCK/LIGHTTRAVELER

LOCAL DIALECT

AN INTRODUCTION TO SCOUSE!

THE LIVERPOOL DIALECT, known across the country as Scouse, is one of the few regional dialects that is active, vibrant and growing while others are threatened with extinction. It is a heady mix of Lancashire, Irish, Scots and Welsh with dashes of many other national and international tongues, the result of Liverpool's long maritime and trading history.

The Scouse dialect as we recognise it today was once confined to certain areas of the city populated mainly by the poor, but the slum clearances of areas such as Speke during the twentieth century and the influx of "Liverpool Irish" to other areas of the city resulted in the rapid spread of the speech patterns and the dialect's continued evolution. There is a rough rule of thumb that the dialect becomes weaker with increasing distance from the waterfront, and indeed there are variations, with Scousers from the southern side of the city having a softer and more lyrical pattern in comparison with the northern areas, where the speech is harder and grittier. The rising inflections at the end of sentences and the sing-song lilt, the result of the Irish influence, give the dialect an irrepressible optimism and good humour.

Native Scouse speakers are renowned for their down-to-earth honesty and rapid speech, but most of all for their no-holds-barred humour. This is both personal and inoffensive, with affectionate jibes aimed at each other and the city as well as foreigners (woolybacks); for instance, the new Roman Catholic cathedral, originally designed by Lutyens and finished (to a revised design) in the 1960s for the increasing numbers of Irish Catholics, is known as Paddy's Wigwam because of its conical design, and the world-renowned Royal Liverpool Philharmonic, founded in 1841 and the oldest surviving professional orchestra in the UK, is known locally as Tut's Band because the design of the Liverpool Philharmonic Hall is said to be based on the decoration in the Pharaoh Tutankhamen's tomb in the Valley of the Kings in Egypt.

Similarly, the Liverpool Overhead Railway was a great innovation in its time, being the world's first electric elevated railway. It was opened in 1893 to carry passengers around the Liverpool Docks without interfering with road and goods traffic below, and it represented a number of technological breakthroughs and experimental techniques.

However, it was known locally (and rather irreverently) as the Dockers' Umbrella, because dock workers were able to walk about the docks under the raised sections of rail and avoid rain and other inclement weather.

The dialect continues to evolve into the new century, with old pronunciations and usages evolving into new ones influenced by estuary English and received pronunciation from the media. However, this evolution is two-way, with words and phrases from the Scouse dialect making their way into wider usage and influencing the speech of the UK and the world. As a result, in the dictionary which follows, many of the words are easily recognisable and appear in common usage across the rest of the UK; the intention here is to indicate their provenance in the speech of Liverpudlians down the years.

A SCOUSE DICTIONARY

A

Ackers – money or cash
Acting the goat – to behave like an idiot
Allus – always
Alright? – common greeting
Are-eh! – exclamation of disgust, disappointment or disbelief
Auld, ald – old
Away with the mixer – not entirely there, not quite right in the head

B

Bail – leave, exit
Barney – an argument
Batter – hit, fight, punch
Beak – a judge
Beaut – an idiot
Bevvie – an alcoholic drink, usually beer
Bevied up – rather the worse for wear after some alcoholic beverages
Bezzie – best friend, best mate
Biddies – head lice or nits
Bifter – cigarette
Bill, billy – a loner
Bizzies – the police
Blag – a lie
Blert – a lightweight or ineffectual person, usually from outside Liverpool
Boff – to pass wind
Bone orchard – cemetery
Boss – excellent, marvellous, the best
Boxer – a coffin-maker
Bricking it – very worried, scared or anxious
Butty – sandwich

C

Chest – someone who has clearly spent far too much time at the gym
Chuck – food, or more specifically bread
Chuffed – happy. To be dead chuffed is to be very happy
Clobber – clothes
Cob on – to have a cob on is to be a bit depressed or sad
Cock-eyed – wonky, askew, aslant
Council pop – water
Crogger or backie – a passenger ride on the crossbar or handlebars of a bicycle

D

De' – the
Dead – very, extremely
Deffo – definitely, certainly
Dem – them
Desert wellies – sandals
Diddy – small, tiny
Divvie – a stupid person
Do one – run away, make a swift exit
Dosh – money

F

de' Fabs – the Beatles
Fades – damaged (and therefore cheap) goods. Often applied to apples
Fire bobbie – a fireman

G

Gartons – a handkerchief. (Snot rag backwards!)
Gear – the best, the top of the range
Giz, gizzit – give that to me, please
Goz, gozzie – look, view
Grotty – shortened version of grotesque. Dirty, unpleasant, ugly

J

Jarg – counterfeit, fake or of poor quality
Jigger – a back alley. Hence jigger-rabbit – a stray cat, often found hanging about in back alleys
Judy – a girl or woman

K

Kaylied – drunk
Kecks – trousers
Kidda – term of endearment for a younger friend or relation
Kirkby kiss – a headbutt
Knock-off – stolen
Know worra mean? – useful addition to the end of any sentence
Kopite – a supporter of Liverpool FC

L

La' – shortened form of lad, often appended to the end of sentences for emphasis or to draw the attention of the listener
Leg it – run away, escape

M

Made up – very happy, delighted
Meff – a smelly, badly dressed person

N

Narked – upset, unhappy
No-mark – insignificant, useless person
No need – an exclamation of disapproval
Nouse – intelligence, common sense

O

Ocker – a shilling
Ollies – marbles
Our kid – an affectionate term used to refer to children, or sometimes close friends
Ozzie – hospital

P

Paddy's wigwam (or the Mersey Funnel) – the Roman Catholic cathedral completed in the 1960s
Pass-commentable – term used to describe someone who often makes negative comments about others

Q

Queen – an affectionate term for a woman or girl

S

Sag off – play truant from school
Scally – a rogue. Shortened form of scallywag
Scouse – the local dialect, as well as the city's signature dish. From lobscouse, a dish brought to Merseyside by Scandinavian sailors
Scouser – one of the chosen few
Scouser's dozen – a quantity of fifteen of something
Scran – food
Scratch – signing on to collect the dole
Screw – to burgle
Skinny – sly or unfair
Soft lad – an affectionate term for an idiot or fool
Sound – fair, right, proper
Sub – a loan, usually of money

T

Ta-rah – goodbye
Thingy – a useful all-purpose word, often employed when the speaker doesn't really know how to describe what they mean
Trabs – sports shoes or trainers
Twirly – an old lady, a female pensioner

W

West – peculiar, unusual, a bit mad
Wet nelly – a weakling, a weedy person, and also a traditional pudding made from leftover bread or cake
Woolybacks – sheep, or else a derogatory term for those poor folk unfortunate enough to have been born outside Merseyside

Y

Ye wha'? – excuse me? Pardon?
Yez/yous – plural, you folk over there
Yocker – to spit

HUMOUR

A COLLECTION OF RIB-TICKLING JOKES FROM LIVERPOOL

A Scouser friend of mine was applying for a loan. I asked him if he had had difficulty filling in the application form.

"No, not at all," he replied. "It was fine – I've got a great credit rating, I reckon I'll walk it."

"What are you talking about?" I said. "You're from Liverpool. You'll never walk a loan."

A Scouser walks into a tailor's shop.

"Alright, mate," he says. "What's the cheapest suit in the shop?"

The tailor sniffs. "You're wearing it, sir."

Harry proudly drove his new convertible into Liverpool city centre and parked it on the main street.

He was on his way to the recycling centre to get rid of an unwanted gift, a foot spa, which he had put on the back seat.

He was half way to the recycling centre when he realised that he had left the car's top down ... and the foot spa was still on the back seat.

He ran all the way back to his car, but it was too late ... another five foot spas had been dumped in the car.

A Scouser had an accident in his car, colliding with a bollard by the side of the road. The car was not badly damaged, but he decided to make an insurance claim. He phoned his insurers, and answered all the questions as best he could.

The insurance man asked, "Sir, where did the accident occur?"

"On Park Road, in Toxteth."

"Was there any other traffic on the road?"

"No, it was quiet."

"And what gear were you in at the time of the impact?"

A short silence, and then the answer came: "A Nike tracksuit and Reeboks."

A Scouser and his wife walked past a swanky new restaurant in Liverpool city centre. "Did you smell that food?" the woman asked. "Wonderful!"

Being the kind hearted, generous man that he was, her husband thought, "What the hell, I'll treat her!"

So they turned round and walked past it a second time.

A little lad asks his mum where his new Man City shirt is.

"I washed it, son. It's out drying on the line," she replies.

The boy rushes to the window to see his beloved City shirt lying in the mud.

"Mum! Why is my City shirt in the mud?"

Furious, his mum looks out of the window and shouts, "The thieving gits have nicked the pegs again!"

How many Manchester United fans does it take to change a light bulb?

None, they're all happy living in Liverpool's shadow!

A woman who is four months pregnant has an accident and falls into a deep coma. Six months later she wakes up, and her first question is to ask the nearest doctor about the fate of her baby.

"You had twins, a boy and a girl, and they are both fine," says the doctor. "Your brother named them for you."

"Oh no, not my brother! He's from Liverpool! What did he call the girl?"

"Denise," the doctor replies.

That isn't so bad, she thinks, so she asks, "What did he call the boy?"

The doctor answers, "Denephew."

A Liverpool fan spends all his time following the club – he goes to home games and away games, he reads all the club news, and he spends all his free time hanging out with fellow fans talking about the club. His nagging wife becomes more and more exasperated, and eventually she loses her temper.

"It's always Liverpool this, Liverpool that!" she wails. "Sometimes I think you love Liverpool more than you love me!"

The man glares at her in fury. "Woman, sometimes I love Everton more than I love you!"

A man from Knotty Ash was busy digging on his allotment when he glanced up and noticed the local vicar standing on the footpath watching him work. Straightening up and leaning on his spade, the man raised his hand in greeting.

The vicar smiled and gestured at the beautifully tended rows of vegetables on the allotment. "You and God have certainly created a beautiful spot together," he said.

"You're right there, vicar," replied the

man," but between you and me, you should have seen the state of the place when he had it all to himself."

Barry and Mick hadn't seen each other in years. They ran into each other in a pub one night and had a long chat, catching up and telling each other all about their lives. Finally Barry invited Mick to visit him in his new flat in Sefton. "I have a wife and three kids, and they'd love to meet you."

"Great!" replied Mick. "Where do you live?"

Barry scribbled down the address on a beermat. "Here you go. There's plenty of parking behind the flat. Park your car and come around to the front door. Kick it open with your foot, go to the lift and press the button with your left elbow. When you get to the sixth floor, go down the hall until you see my name on the door. Then press the doorbell with your right elbow and I'll let you in."

"Great. But tell me ... what's all this business of kicking the front door open, then pressing the lift buttons with my elbows?"

Barry looked shocked. "Surely you're not coming empty-handed?"

RECIPES

MOUTH-WATERING MEALS FROM LIVERPOOL

Scouse

SHUTTERSTOCK/NEIL LANGAN

See **page 26** for recipe

Wet Nelly

WET NELLY

As well as being a Scouse name for a weedy or ineffectual person, wet nelly is a traditional Liverpool pudding made of leftover bread, biscuits or pastries, compressed and soaked in milk, syrup or honey with spices and dried fruit added. As with scouse there is no exact recipe; the ingredients are flexible, depending on what is available in the store cupboard.

INGREDIENTS:

1 loaf of day-old white bread, crusts cut off and cubed
100g butter
140g brown sugar
350ml milk, warmed
500g mixed dried fruit
1 dsp mixed spice
3 medium eggs

PREPARATION:

1. Soak the bread in the warmed milk for at least four hours, preferably overnight.

2. When fully soaked, add all the other ingredients, mix well and pour into a well greased deep roasting tin.

3. Bake at 180°C, gas 4 for one to one-and-a-half hours, checking regularly after one hour. The wet nelly is done when the surface is springy to the touch.

4. Serve warm with custard or cold with butter and a brew.

Liverpool Tart

LIVERPOOL TART

Invented in 1897 as a rival to the better known Bakewell and Manchester tarts, Liverpool tart is a rich lemony confection sold in bakeries around Merseyside. The recipe, which originally called for 'moist sugar' and 'boiled lemon', has been updated for modern cooks, and there are even Liver Bird pastry cutters available to decorate the tarts.

INGREDIENTS:
One packet of ready-made sweet shortcrust pastry
225g dark Muscovado sugar
50g butter
1 egg
1 unwaxed lemon

PREPARATION:

1. Roll out the pastry and use it to line two four-hole Yorkshire pudding tins (giving eight tarts in total). Reserve some pastry for decorating the tops.

2. Melt the butter and sugar, and then allow to cool but not set.

3. Cut the lemon into small pieces and remove the pips. Put in a blender and shred until fine.

4. Beat the butter/sugar mixture and the shredded lemon together with the egg, and pour into the pastry cases.

5. If you wish, use the leftover pastry to decorate the tops – either with twisted strips to form a lattice, or using a cutter to make shapes.

6. Bake at 190°C, gas 5 for 17 to 20 minutes. Decorate with sifted icing sugar. Serve warm with custard, or cold with a good strong cup of tea.

SCOUSE

Scouse, originally called lobscouse, is the 'national' dish of Liverpool, a hearty warming stew brought to the city by Scandinavian sailors and made from cheap and cheerful ingredients. Every Liverpool family has its own recipe, often adapted based on what was available; here is one that won't fail to please.

INGREDIENTS:

1 carrot, peeled and chopped
2 onions, peeled and chopped
5 medium white potatoes, peeled and cut into chunks
300g lamb neck fillets, cut into chunks with the fat removed
Freshly ground black pepper
Pinch of salt
A dash of Worcestershire sauce
Stock cube

PREPARATION:

1. Slightly brown off the lamb in a frying pan. Transfer it to a large pan and add the chopped vegetables, covering with hot water.

2. Season with salt and black pepper, add the stock cube and Worcestershire sauce, cover and bring to the boil.

3. Reduce the heat and keep the pan at a low simmer for around one-and-a-half to two hours. The timing needn't be exact, but keep checking and stirring from time to time. The scouse is done when the potatoes and carrots are soft and the meat is tender.

4. Serve in bowls with pickled red cabbage or beetroot, and/or with some crusty white bread. 'Blind' or vegetarian scouse may be made by omitting the meat and Worcestershire sauce, and true Scousers often use cold leftover scouse in their butties!

MURDERS

NOTORIOUS MURDERS ON THE STREETS OF LIVERPOOL

THE SIXPENNY MURDER

On 3rd August 1874, a Bank Holiday Monday, Richard Morgan was walking down Tithebarn Street with his wife Alice and brother Samuel. They had been to the New Ferry Gala and were walking home from the landing stage when they passed a group of youths gathered on a street corner. These 'cornermen' were members of the High Rip Gang which terrorised northern Liverpool at that time. One of them, John McCrave, demanded sixpence in ale money.

Richard retorted that if he found a job McCrave could pay for his own ale, whereupon McCrave attacked him

from behind, knocking him sprawling into the road. There followed a brutal gang attack, with Samuel and Alice vainly trying to shield Richard's body from the rain of punches and kicks. Alice was kicked in the head, leaving her deaf.

Alice screamed for the police and a crowd gathered, but far from helping Richard the onlookers encouraged the attack and some even joined in. Richard's lifeless body was kicked some fifteen metres down the street before the police arrived and the gang dispersed.

Samuel pursued McCrave and he was arrested later that evening, with two others, Michael Mullen and Peter Campbell, apprehended within days. All three were found guilty of murder; McCrave and Mullen were hanged at Kirkdale, and Campbell received life imprisonment. The case brought the serious gang problems of Liverpool to public attention for the first time.

THE BABIES IN THE BOXES

Elizabeth Kirkbride was a quiet, genteel woman who was born and educated in Everton in the 1830s or 1840s. She married young and lived in Litherland, but her husband died leaving her in straightened circumstances with two sons. She became a school mistress and lived with her parents in Penrith for a time, but returned to Liverpool in 1876 with her sons to live quietly in Tuebrook, West Derby.

However, in early 1877 a shocking discovery was made. A box which Elizabeth had left in a hotel storeroom in Penrith was opened when a disagreeable smell was noticed, and it was found to contain the badly decomposed bodies of two infants. She was immediately arrested in Liverpool, and a search of her rooms turned up three more infant bodies, all dead for some years and stored in a trunk. Her son admitted to finding the body of a sixth infant at their home in Penrith and burying it in the garden.

Elizabeth admitted concealing the births and the bodies, but claimed she had not murdered the children. However, at least one of the babies had a ligature round its neck. She named an accomplice – her lover Thomas Moss, a successful businessman from Penrith who had promised to marry her but instead had married another. However, he was never arraigned or brought to court.

The case became a cause celebre, and Elizabeth's appearance at the bar in February 1877 caused riots outside the court. She was sentenced to two years and three months' hard labour – nine months for each of three charges of concealment of birth, since murder could not be proved.

THE BLACK WIDOWS OF LIVERPOOL

In the early 1880s two unmarried sisters, Catherine and Margaret Flannagan, ran a boarding house on Skirving Street, providing lodgings for Catherine's son John as well as two widowers and their daughters – Thomas and Mary Higgins, and Patrick and Margaret Jennings.

John died suddenly in 1880 at the age of 22, and his mother collected £71 from the burial society. Margaret Flannagan married Thomas Higgins in 1882, but within months Thomas' daughter Mary, aged 8, had also died.

MARGARET HIGGINS
CREATIVE COMMONS

CATHERINE FLANNAGAN
CREATIVE COMMONS

Again the burial society paid out to the grieving stepmother.

A few months later Margaret Jennings died; she was 19, and this time the burial payment was collected by Catherine. Local society was beginning to notice the high death rate, and the household moved several times. In September 1883 Thomas Higgins fell ill and was diagnosed with dysentery; he died after two days of illness.

Higgins' brother Patrick was suspicious that Thomas, a previously healthy man, had succumbed so quickly, and he began to investigate. He discovered that Thomas had been insured with five different burial societies, and his widow Margaret stood to profit by about £100. An autopsy was ordered, and both sisters were arrested when lethal quantities of arsenic were found in Higgins' body. Arsenic was found in the house and in Margaret's pockets, and also in the exhumed bodies of John Flannagan, Mary Higgins and

Margaret Jennings. The sisters were found guilty of the murder of Thomas Higgins, and were hanged on the same day in 1884.

However, perhaps the most disturbing thing was Catherine's assertion that these murders were not isolated; in fact, she claimed there was an extended ring of women who had either committed similar murders or paid out insurance for them. These claims could not be proven, but the suspicion remains that Catherine and Margaret Flannagan were not the only Black Widows of Liverpool.

THE PROTESTANT MARTYR

John Kensit was born in 1853 in London, some thirty years after the Catholic Emancipation Act which restored Roman Catholicism to a place in public life. He developed fervent Protestant beliefs and founded the Protestant Truth Society with the aim of keeping the Church of England separate from Roman Catholic influence.

In 1989, infuriated by the failure of the Church to act against the adoption of Roman Catholic practices, he took to travelling the country as a Protestant lecturer and agitator denouncing ritualism in the Church. He led a band of itinerant preachers known as "Wicliffites", who would enter churches which they believed had adopted

John Kensit CREATIVE COMMONS

ritualistic practices and disrupt services. Kensit himself was fined for brawling in church, and he was famous for his public protests and denunciations of clergymen.

In 1902 he and his followers attended a peaceful public meeting at the Claughton Music Hall in Birkenhead. Afterwards on the short walk to the Birkenhead Ferry Kensit and his party passed a group of young people, one of whom threw a heavy iron chisel. It struck Kensit on the forehead and he collapsed to the ground. He was rushed to hospital, but died two weeks later of pneumonia and blood poisoning.

A young man called John McKeever was charged with murder, but the evidence was conflicting and he was acquitted in December 1902. Kensit was buried in Hampstead, and is remembered as the first Protestant martyr, who paid the ultimate price for standing up for his beliefs when bishops and clergymen failed to do so.

WHO KILLED JULIA WALLACE?

The murder of Julia Wallace in 1931 remains one of Liverpool's most baffling unsolved cases. Julia, who was married to William Wallace, an insurance agent, was brutally bludgeoned to death in the front parlour of their home while William was out, apparently called to the other side of the city on a fool's errand by an anonymous caller.

The police were suspicious of William's report of a mysterious and evidently non-existent Mr Qualtrough who had telephoned him at his Chess Club with a promise of business, and set out to test his story. They noted the last time that Julia was seen alive, and then made various "tram tests", riding the trams to determine whether William would have had time to murder his wife and then travel across the city to the locations where he was seen and spoken to by witnesses.

Julia Wallace CREATIVE COMMONS

After many tests they determined that it was possible for William to have committed the murder, and he was arrested. However, the tests were based on the travelling times of young fit policemen walking briskly between tram stops, not on the speed of an unfit man in his fifties. William was found guilty and sentenced to death, but was released after the Court of Appeal decided the verdict could not be supported. William died in 1933 and was buried with his wife.

So who did make the call, and who murdered Julia? Suspicion falls on Richard Gordon Parry, a junior employee at William's insurance firm. Parry was also a petty criminal who knew that William kept a cash box at his home, and there is some suggestion that the police suppressed evidence of a blood-stained glove found in Parry's car. However, Parry died in 1980, and it is likely that the mystery of who killed Julia Wallace will never be solved.

THE CAMEO CINEMA MURDERS

The Cameo Cinema murders in March 1949 have been the subject of considerable controversy. On the evening of 19 March 1949 the manager of the Cameo Cinema, Leonard Thomas, and his deputy Bernard Catterall were counting the day's

Cameo Cinema CREATIVE COMMONS

takings in the cinema office when a masked and armed man burst in. Thomas and Catterall refused to hand over the bag of cash so the man shot them both, wounding them fatally. After threatening other members of staff the man made his escape empty-handed, sprinting away down an alley.

A city-wide manhunt bore no fruit until a letter from a prostitute and her pimp revealed the names of two men, Charles Connolly and George Kelly. Both protested their innocence and had sound alibis for the evening of 19 March, but nevertheless they were arrested and charged with the murders.

They stood trial together on 12 January 1950, but the jury failed to reach a verdict and separate retrials were ordered. Kelly was tried first, found guilty and sentenced to death, and then Connolly pleaded guilty when faced with the choice between execution or a commutation of his sentence. Kelly was executed on 28 March 1950; Connolly was released from prison in 1957 and died in 1997. Both men insisted on their innocence until the end.

There have been a number of attempts to re-open the case, citing unreliable witnesses, threats and inducements, tampering with evidence, and the fact that another man, a convicted criminal, apparently admitted to complicity in the murders before Kelly and Connolly were even arrested. The case finally came before the Court of Appeal in February 2001, and Kelly's and Connolly's convictions were judged unsafe and duly quashed.

LOCAL NAMES

THE STANLEY FAMILY

The Stanley family have been connected with Liverpool and west Lancashire for hundreds of years. Coming from humble origins, the family name was once de Audley, but it was changed to Stanley in the twelfth century when Adam de Stanley was granted the manor of Stoneleigh (Stanley) in Staffordshire. From there the family inherited huge estates through the marriage of Sir John Stanley to Isabel Lathom, and the Stanleys (later Earls of Derby) went on to become major landowners throughout the northwest and as far afield as the Isle of Man. Lord Thomas Stanley, the first Earl, became known as the Kingmaker at the Battle of Bosworth in August 1485, when legend states he plucked the crown of England from a hawthorn bush after the death of King Richard III and placed it on the head of his stepson, the victorious Henry Tudor, soon to be crowned Henry VII.

The Stanley family home was and remains Knowsley Hall, but the family used to own and live in the Tower of Liverpool, built in 1256 on the shores of the Mersey.

Thomas Stanley 1st Earl of Derby

Originally a sandstone mansion, the building was remodelled when it was acquired by the Stanley family and became a fortress in the heart of the city. It was demolished in 1819, and the site opposite the Royal Liver Building is now occupied by the

Tower Buildings, a commercial property. The Stanley name occurs often in the Liverpool area in pubs and street names, and Stanleys are also present in the family trees of some of the city's most famous sons, most notably John Lennon.

THE MOLYNEUX FAMILY

The ancestors of the Molyneux family arrived around the time of the Norman conquest in 1066, bearing the name de Molines. They were present at the Battle of Hastings and were rewarded by William of Normandy with lands in Lancashire; they became the Earls of Sefton, and their family home was at Croxteth Hall.

Croxteth Hall CREATIVE COMMONS

Sir Richard Molyneux was appointed Constable of Liverpool Castle in 1440, which brought to a head the family feud with the Stanleys, Earls of Derby, who owned the Tower of Liverpool just down the road. There was fighting in the streets between supporters of the two families, with bands of men attacking the stronghold of the opposing faction.

Peace was only restored by the Sheriff of Lancashire acting on behalf of the King. The family were staunch Catholics, siding firmly with the King during the Civil War. However, in 1643 Parliamentarian forces took control of the town and Lord Molyneux was forced to retreat to Liverpool Castle, from where he was eventually driven out of town along with other Royalists. The castle was finally destroyed in 1715. The Earldom of Sefton became extinct in 1972 when the seventh and final Earl died without an heir. Croxteth Hall now belongs to the City Council, and is open to the public.

WALKS

CITY STREETS AND DOCKLAND WALKS

LIVERPOOL TOWN CENTRE
2.5 miles approx

Start by the entrance of the Metropolitan Cathedral (RC). From the top of the steps there is a fine view back along Hope Street to the Anglican Cathedral. Head along Mount Pleasant until you reach Brownlow Hill where Liverpool University's grand red-brick Victorian building stands on the opposite corner. Cross over Brownlow Hill into Ashton Street and turn left through an archway into the secluded quadrangle at the rear of the Victoria Building.

Bear round to the left to return to Brownlow Hill. Walk down to the bottom of the hill where Mount

Metropolitan Cathedral ANDY/SUSAN CAFFREY

Pleasant joins from the left. On your right at the junction is Liverpool's' famous Adelphi Hotel; turn right in front of the Adelphi along Lime Street where you pass two magnificent Edwardian pubs, The Vines and The Crown. Further along is Lime Street Station. Cross in front of the station to the first of Liverpool's famous group of neo-classical masterpieces, St. George's Hall. Go up the steps and walk along the plateau towards Wellington's Column and the Steble Fountain. In front of you is the spectacular array of buildings on William Brown Street - the County Sessions House, the Walker Art Gallery, the Picton Reading Room, the William Brown Library and Museum. Walk down William Brown Street and enter St. John's Gardens. Exit the gardens at the other side and cross over to Queen Square, which is full of restaurants and bars. Keep ahead to the bus station and cross over into Williamson Square which is

St. George's Hall ANDY/SUSAN CAFFREY

TOWN CENTRE **WALK** 39

The William Brown Library and Museum ANDY/SUSAN CAFFREY

dominated by a water sculpture and the Playhouse Theatre on the left. Cross the square diagonally to locate Tarleton Street at the opposite corner. Go along Tarleton Street and turn left onto Church Street and immediately right into Church Alley, at the end of which is Bluecoat Chambers, the oldest surviving building in the centre of the city. Retrace your steps and turn right up Church Street, crossing over into Bold Street. At the top turn right into Berry Sreet and take the third turning on the left (Knight Street). Continue ahead into Mount Street, then turn left onto Hope Street. Next left is Rice Street with a curious pub called 'Ye Cracke' - worth a visit. Continue along Hope Street towards the Metropolitan Cathedral. On the right at Myrtle Street is the Philharmonic Hall, and on the opposite corner is one of Liverpool's most famous pubs, the Philharmonic Dining Rooms.

The Philharmonic Dining Rooms ANDY/SUSAN CAFFREY

Return to Hope Street and continue ahead to return to your starting point at the Cathedral.

The Three Graces ANDY/SUSAN CAFFREY

WATERFRONT WALK
2 miles approx

Start on Canada Boulevard at the Pier Head, taking in the splendour of the Three Graces: the Royal Liver Building, the Cunard Building and the Port of Liverpool Building, noting the Leeds and Liverpool canal extension to the Albert Dock which runs elegantly through. This is a good place to watch the famous Mersey Ferries come and go. When ready, make your way to

Piermaster's House ANDY/SUSAN CAFFREY

The historic lightship 'Planet' ANDY/SUSAN CAFFREY

the Piermaster's House which is at the entrance to the dock area. Proceed past the Tate Gallery and explore the Albert Dock with its many shops, restaurants, museums and the Beatles Story. When you have finished here, make your way to the Strand with the bright red historic lightship 'Planet' close to the pedestrian lights. Cross here and head up the steps opposite into the Liverpool One shopping development and Chavasse Park. Head along the lower level towards John Lewis and turn left into Paradise Street. Continue into Whitechapel, looking out for tiny Button Street on the left, and

The Dock area ANDY/SUSAN CAFFREY

Button St. ANDY/SUSAN CAFFREY

The White Star pub ANDY/SUSAN CAFFREY

turn into it. Go right at the fork in the street, past a fine old pub called the White Star and then left into Matthew Street. This is the centre of the Beatles universe! With the reconstructed Cavern Club and another great pub, The Grapes, which was one

The Grapes pub ANDY/SUSAN CAFFREY

of the Beatles' haunts in the sixties. At the end of Matthew Street, turn right into North John Street, crossing over Victoria Street. On the corner with Dale Street is the lofty Royal Insurance Building with its golden dome. Opposite is the old pub Rigbys. Cross Dale Street to Hackins Hey

Ye Hole in Ye Wall ANDY/SUSAN CAFFREY

and find Ye Hole in Ye Wall, which dates from 1706 and lays claim to being Liverpool's oldest pub. Emerge from Hackins Hey left onto Tithebarn Street and continue down into Chapel Street. Turn left into the church yard

WATERFRONT **WALK** 43

of Our Lady and St Nicholas with its delightful gardens and proceed through to Water Street. Turn right and pick up the Strand. Turn left along the Strand to James Street to find the curious streaky bacon-patterned White Star Line offices on the corner.

George's Dock Ventilation and Control Station
ANDY/SUSAN CAFFREY

The White Star Line offices ANDY/SUSAN CAFFREY

Cross Strand Street via the pedestrian lights and turn to the right past the huge George's Dock Ventilation and Control Station (for the Birkenhead Road Tunnel) and the magnificent Tower Buildings. Return around the rear of the Royal Liver Building to the start of the walk.

GHOST STORIES

GHOSTLY GOINGS ON IN LIVERPOOL...

THE HITCHHIKER IN THE QUEENSWAY TUNNEL

The two-mile-long Queensway or Birkenhead Tunnel was constructed between 1925 and 1934, to carry road traffic beneath the Mersey between Liverpool and Birkenhead. During its construction seventeen men were killed, and since then it has gathered a reputation for apparitions and hauntings.

The figure of a woman has been reported to stand in the centre of the carriageway in front of oncoming cars, seemingly in an attempt to cause accidents; indeed, several drivers have swerved to avoid her and been involved in collisions as a result. The

Queensway Tunnel MIKE PENNINGTON

GHOST **STORIES** 45

ghost is thought to be of a girl who was a pillion passenger on a motorcycle in the 1960s, who fell off and was killed in the tunnel. Another apparition, possibly the same woman, has been seen hitchhiking along the length of the tunnel on various occasions.

The tunnel has also been reported to be the site of time slips, with old-fashioned police cars and futuristic golden vehicles spotted driving along its length and occasionally vanishing into the wall.

BLOODY ACRE, CHILDWALL

Many tales surround the aptly named Bloody Acre in Childwall, which supposedly gets its name either from the reddish colour of the soil and vegetation in the summer months, or else from the blood spilled during a skirmish (some say a massacre) in the 1640s during the Civil War. Cannon balls have reportedly been dug up in the gardens of nearby houses, although the Acre itself has never been built on or excavated. In the daylight hours the field, adjacent to All Saints Church and cemetery in Childwall, is frequented by dog walkers, but once night has fallen passers-by have reported hearing the sounds of battle – men and women shouting, the clash of weapons, musket fire and the groans of the dying.

In the 1960s a pair of policemen on the Childwall beat were alerted by a group of children and they all witnessed a strange apparition of a barefoot bearded man in white robes standing outside the All Saints church gates. As they approached him he vanished in front of their eyes, and it was later discovered that a disturbed grave in the nearby cemetery contained remains very reminiscent of the man they had seen.

ST JAMES CEMETERY

William Huskisson is one of many ghosts said to haunt St James Cemetery, a splendidly gothic former quarry where 57,000 people were reportedly buried between 1825 and 1936. Huskisson, born in Staffordshire in 1770, was a statesman, financier and Member of Parliament for Liverpool. In September 1830 he proudly attended the opening of the Liverpool and Manchester Railway, setting off from Liverpool in the same train as the Duke of Wellington.

The locomotives stopped to take on water at Parkside, mid-way between Liverpool and Manchester, and despite warnings from railway staff, many of the dignitaries and other passengers chose to disembark. Huskisson approached the Duke of Wellington's carriage, hoping for a reconciliation after a disagreement which had caused him to resign from the Cabinet. However, he failed to notice George Stevenson's Rocket locomotive approaching on another line until it was too late; panicking, he tried to climb into the Duke's carriage to escape, but the door swung open and deposited him on the tracks directly in front of the oncoming engine. His legs were terribly damaged, and he died a few hours later in hospital (after being transported there in another steam train).

The shade of this first fatality of the railway system can, it seems, still be heard walking around the monument which was erected to his memory in St James Cemetery, and which still stands there even though the cemetery is now a public park.

SPEKE HALL

Grey ladies are reportedly women who had died for love, and Speke Hall, a timber-framed Tudor manor house on the banks of the Mersey, has its very own. Mary Norris, the daughter and heiress of Thomas Norris MP, married the notorious rake and fortune hunter Lord Sidney Beauclerk in 1736. Sidney was an inveterate gambler with a definite eye for the ladies, once described as 'Nell Gwyn in person, with the sex altered' – Mary's marriage cannot have been entirely happy.

The story goes that after one particularly disastrous gambling session Sidney was forced to tell Mary that he had lost most of their worldly possessions. Distraught, she lost her

The north front of Speke Hall, Merseyside NATIONAL TRUST/ANDREW BUTLER

wits and flung their infant son from an upstairs window into the moat, where he drowned. Realising what she had done she then killed herself, and can now sometimes be seen and heard in the Tapestry Room or rocking a cradle in the Oak Bedroom.

This tale does not entirely match the historical facts, however, since Mary and Sidney's son Topham actually lived to a good age, marrying the daughter of the Duke of Marlborough and becoming a friend of Samuel Johnson. Nevertheless, a similar tale might explain the spooky phenomena. This story records that the tragic story of the baby falling from the window actually occurred in a failed escape attempt during the Civil War, when the house was besieged by Parliamentarian forces. The unknown lady is now doomed to wander Speke Hall searching for her lost child.

THE ADELPHI HOTEL

The Adelphi Hotel in Ranelagh Place was once described as 'the most luxurious hotel outside London', and was a favoured stopping-off point for wealthy passengers travelling on the cruise liners between Liverpool and the US. Politicians, public figures and famous artists appearing at Liverpool's theatres also stayed here; over the years the guests have included Winston Churchill, Frank Sinatra, Laurel and Hardy and Judy Garland.

Any building with such a long history is bound to contain a few echoes of the past, and the Adelphi is no exception. Guests have reported the figure of a man – some suggest he is dressed in military uniform of the First World War era – standing by their beds. The man is nicknamed George, and the stories suggest he likes to observe out-of-towners come to Liverpool for the Grand National.

being watched during their stay. Voices have been heard coming from empty rooms, disembodied screams have woken guests, and it has been reported that the hotel's staff avoid going into certain suites on the first floor if they can help it because of the unexplained activity and unpleasant feelings in those rooms.

THEATRE GHOSTS

Theatres are always fertile locations for ghostly goings on, and Liverpool's theatres are no exception. The Liverpool Playhouse is haunted by the shade of a cleaner named Elizabeth, who was sweeping the stage in 1897 when the fire curtain came down and knocked her into the orchestra pit, breaking her neck. She haunts the gallery level, sometimes sitting in seat A5. Workmen refurbishing the theatre in 1999 reportedly downed tools because of all the inexplicable events, such as taps being turned on and off and heavy doors slamming shut. A

Adelphi Hotel SUE ADAIRE

Other stories tell of a phantom chambermaid who wakes guests, particularly on the fifth floor, and many people have reported feeling ill, experiencing cold spots in their rooms or feeling as if they were

GHOST **STORIES** 51

grey lady and a Victorian gentleman have also been seen in the stalls and the bar area.

The Liverpool Empire is haunted by a young girl who appears to be about ten years old. She appears late at night in the stalls, and often seems to be upset; she has been seen being dragged away by a male figure, but both of them disappear if they are approached. The suspicion is that the girl fell to her death from the circle into the stalls, but no one is certain who she is.

Caretakers sometimes come back after death to watch over their places of work – or so it seems, since the Empire and the Royal Court both have a resident handyman. Coincidentally both called Les, they are often blamed for mysterious accidents and are sometimes seen around the theatres, keeping an eye on the repairs in the buildings they once worked on.

The Liverpool Empire SHUTTERSTOCK/PAUL J MARTIN

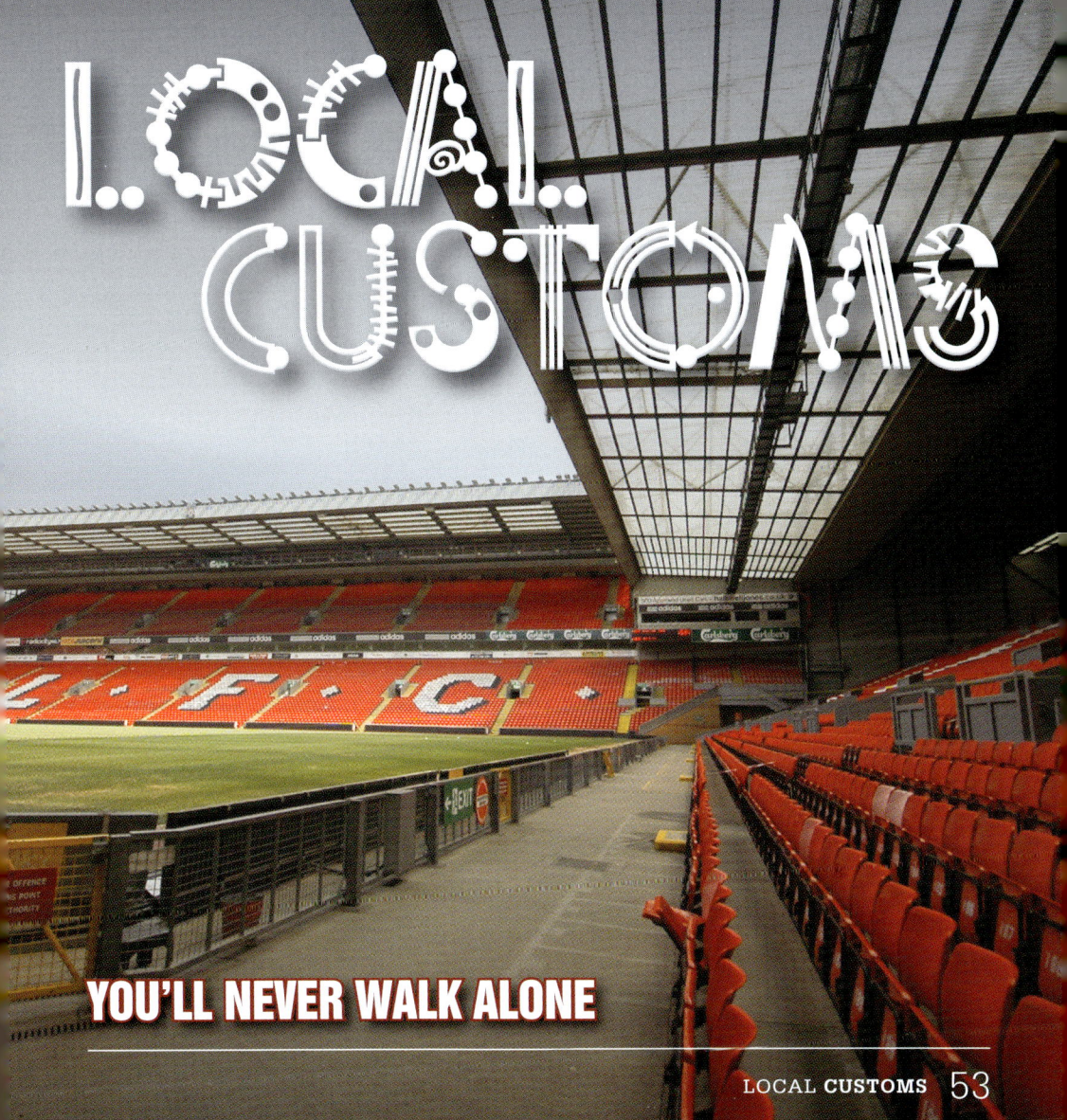

First performed in 1945 in the original Broadway production of Rodgers and Hammerstein's Carousel, *You'll Never Walk Alone* is sung in the musical to comfort and encourage a woman, Julie, whose husband Billy has committed suicide. Later in the show it is reprised by Julie and sung to the couple's daughter Louise as she graduates from college.

There have been many recordings of the song down the years, but the one which is most associated with Liverpool is the cover by Gerry and the Pacemakers from 1963.

The track was recorded at the Abbey Road studios and produced by George Martin, so its Merseybeat provenance is impeccable, and it was quickly adopted by the Liverpool FC supporters as the club's anthem. The story goes that Gerry Marsden gave a recording of the song to Bill Shankly in the summer of 1963, who took it along on a pre-season tour. The players liked the song and journalists on the tour reported that it had been adopted as the club song, and before long it was resounding around the Spion Kop.

Other football clubs around the world have also adopted the song, notably Celtic FC, Feyenoord, Borussia Dortmund and FC Tokyo, but it will always be most associated with Liverpool FC.

The title of the song features in the club's crest and on the Shankly Gate entrance to Anfield, and it is sung in rousing and emotional chorus moments before the start of every home game.

When you walk through the storm
Hold your head up high...

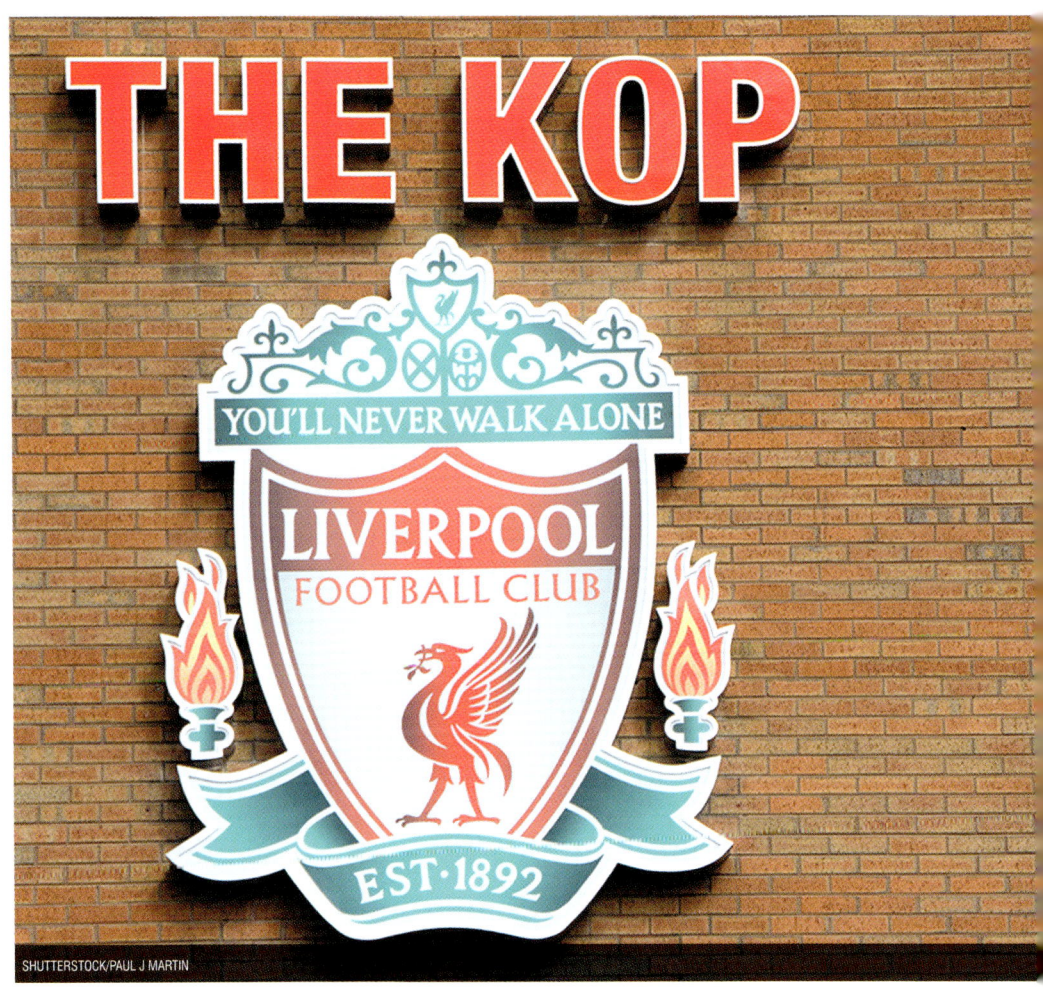

LIVERPOOL CHINATOWN

Liverpool Chinatown is the oldest established Chinatown in Europe. Chinese immigrants first arrived in Liverpool in the 1830s, travelling directly from China to trade in silks, cotton and tea. Some of the traders and mariners brought their families with them or married local women, settling and starting boarding houses and businesses catering to the large numbers of Chinese sailors employed by Alfred Holt and the Blue Funnel Shipping Line. Gradually, strong trade and cultural links developed between Liverpool, Shanghai and Hong Kong.

Chinatown is located in the south of the city near Liverpool Cathedral, although it was originally in the docklands; heavy bombing during World War II caused a relocation of the Chinese cultural centre. The arch at the entrance to the area is a beautiful fifteen-metre multiple-span arch, the biggest of its type outside

China, constructed in Shanghai and assembled in situ in 2000 as a symbol of Liverpool's commitment to regenerate and redevelop what had become a run-down part of the city.

Within the bounds of Chinatown, all the street signs are in Chinese and English, and there is a profusion of Chinese businesses such as restaurants, supermarkets and bookshops, as well as community and religious associations, leisure facilities and voluntary groups. There are Chinese-speaking GPs and dentists and language schools teaching both English and Chinese, and there is also a commemorative plaque dedicated to the thousands of Chinese mariners who served in the British merchant fleet during the First and Second World Wars.

IRISH LINKS

Liverpool has the strongest Irish heritage of any city in the UK. Immigration from Ireland began very early in the city's history, and Irish influence is detectable in the lilting Scouse dialect as well as in the religion and culture of the city.

The most intense period of immigration occurred in the middle of the nineteenth century, with Irish families leaving their homes in droves to escape the potato famine which caused poverty and starvation at home. By the end of the famine in the early 1850s there were around ninety thousand Irish-born people living in Liverpool, and many hundreds of thousands more had passed through on their way to other parts of the UK or further afield to the US and beyond. Most of those who settled in Liverpool were poor, hungry and vulnerable to disease and exploitation, and for a while the city struggled to cope.

The perfect pint GETTYIMAGES

Eventually, however, the city rallied and embraced the newcomers, with Irish dock workers playing a huge role in the development of the docks and the efficiency of trade and transport of goods. Liverpool is the only English city to have a significant Orange Order membership, with many annual parades held across the city during the marching season of June and July.

Many of the city's most famous sons and daughters are of Irish extraction – John Lennon, Paul McCartney and George Harrison, to name but three. Since 2003 there has been an annual Irish Festival, held in October to celebrate Liverpool's links with Ireland and highlight the Irish impact on the city.

LOCAL SPORTS

THE GRAND NATIONAL

The Grand National, the premier National Hunt horse race in the UK, is held in April every year at Aintree Racecourse. It is a handicap steeplechase run over just over four miles, with horses jumping thirty fences over two laps of the course. There is some dispute over the date of the first official Grand National, with some historians favouring a steeplechase in 1836 won by The Duke (ridden by Captain Martin Becher) and some a similar race in 1839 won by Lottery (ridden by Jem Mason), but all agree that the race was founded by William Lynn, a hotelier who leased land in Aintree from the Earl of Sefton and built a racecourse there.

Initially a local affair, the race became truly national with the advent of the railway, and rapidly gained in popularity to become a major event in the sporting calendar. It was moved temporarily to Gatwick during the First World War and suspended from 1941 to 1945, but outside of wartime the race has only ever been declared void once, in 1993, when confusion in the gates caused two false starts. However, several jockeys did not realise the second call-back and continued to race; seven horses completed both laps of the circuit, with Esha Ness coming home the eventual 'winner' of the National that never was.

The fences are notoriously tricky, causing many fallers in bad years; in 1928 the conditions were so difficult that forty-one out of the forty-two starters fell during the race, and only two horses completed the course. The heroic winner that year was Tipperary Tim ridden by William Dutton, who came in at an unlikely 100/1. Another lucky 100/1 winner was Foinavon in 1967, whose jockey John Buckingham took advantage of a massive pile-up to come from a hundred yards back and win the race.

The most successful horse in Grand National history was Red Rum who dominated the race in the mid-1970s, winning in 1973, 1974 and 1977 and finishing second in 1975 and 1976. Reynoldstown won twice in 1935 and 1936; other famous winners in recent years have been Aldaniti (1981, ridden by Bob Champion) and Seagram (1991, ridden by Nigel Hawke).

FOOTBALLING RIVALRIES – LIVERPOOL, EVERTON AND TRANMERE

Football is a serious business on Merseyside; the city of Liverpool is statistically the most successful. Everton FC is the oldest club in the city, founded in 1878 and originally based at Anfield. However, a dispute between the board and the chairman John Houlding (who also owned the ground) resulted in the club moving out in 1892 and purchasing a new ground at Goodison Park, less than a mile from Anfield across Stanley Park. In response Houlding founded his own club, Liverpool FC, and one of football's most enduring rivalries began. The third Merseyside team, Tranmere Rovers, was founded in 1885 and is based at Prenton Park in Birkenhead.

Matches between the Merseyside clubs are always an emotional affair. Fixtures between Liverpool and Everton are known as the 'friendly derby' since so many Merseyside families contain supporters of both teams. The stands are often unsegregated, and Anfield and Goodison, particularly the vocal supporters on Anfield's famous Spion Kop, both resound to the universal chant of "Merseyside! Merseyside!" Unlike derby matches in other cities there is no geographical, political or religious division between the two clubs, but in recent years the rivalry has intensified and the fixture has become increasingly ill-tempered.

Tranmere has existed somewhat in the

shadow of its larger and more famous neighbours. The club has never made it into the top flight, so that competitive matches with Liverpool and Everton are rare. However, there have occasionally been fixtures in cup competitions; in the FA cup in 2001 Tranmere caused a major upset by beating Everton 3-0 in the fourth round, before losing 4-2 to Liverpool in the quarter finals.

THE LIVERPOOL OLYMPICS

The mid-nineteenth century was a time of enormous sporting and entrepreneurial spirit, and nowhere was this more apparent than in the Liverpool Grand Olympic Festivals. These events were organised during the 1860s by John Hulley, a Liverpool-born gymnastics and athletics enthusiast who firmly believed in the benefits of public participation in sport.

The Liverpool Olympic Festivals were held at parade grounds and in the newly-built Liverpool Gymnasium, and included athletics, boxing and gymnastics. The events were very well attended by members of the public, who listened to speeches about the benefits of participation in exercise and sport before watching competitions and displays of exercises and gymnastics. John Hulley himself was always present extolling the virtues of exercise, particularly gymnastics, sea-swimming and cycling; he was responsible for the introduction of the velocipede (a forerunner of the bicycle) to the UK, organising races at Hoylake in 1869.

Hulley was instrumental in the formation of the National Olympic Association, the predecessor of the modern British Olympic Association. He was vociferous about the amateur sportsmanship of the Olympic movement, remaining adamant that professionals (or even semi-professionals) should not be allowed to compete; this is still a central pillar of the Olympic movement today. It is likely that without Hulley and others like him (particularly William Penny Brookes from Much Wenlock in Shropshire), Pierre de Coubertin would not have been inspired to found the International Olympic Committee; Liverpool can justifiably claim to be one of the birthplaces of the modern Olympics.

SHUTTERSTOCK/LYNEA

LOCAL HISTORY

THIS IS THE TIME AND THIS IS THE PLACE!

THE PORT OF LIVERPOOL

Liverpool's first dock was the Old Dock, opened in 1715 and developed from the original tidal pool from which Liverpool derived its name. Engineered by Thomas Steers, the Old Dock was the world's first commercial wet dock, with berths for up to one hundred ships. Active for a little over a century, the Old Dock eventually became too small and was closed and filled in around 1826; the site used to hold the Customs House, and is now part of the Paradise Project.

Over the centuries, from the Old Dock the Liverpool system developed into an extended network of interconnected docks, with both dry and wet docks linked by gates and extending over 7.5 miles along the shores of the Mersey. Many of the smaller docks have been filled in and the land used for commercial or

SHUTTERSTOCK/KENNY1

industrial purposes, but the remaining docks, operated by the Mersey Docks and Harbour Company, still provide facilities for shipbuilders and berths for cruise liners as well as trading vessels and container ships.

In their heyday the docks were served by over 100 miles of railway lines carrying both freight and passengers. Today much of the Port of Liverpool is a World Heritage Site, ensuring that the buildings and structures of the port are preserved and its leading role in the development of dock construction, port management and international trade throughout the eighteenth and nineteenth centuries is recognised.

COMMERCIAL AND INDUSTRIAL HISTORY

Powered by its maritime heritage, Liverpool has a long and proud commercial and industrial history. The city acknowledges that some of this history was built on Liverpool merchants' involvement in the reprehensible slave trade during the eighteenth century, but this was only a relatively small part of the mercantile activity which boosted the city's status. Liverpool merchants also dealt in a wide range of commodities, from local cloth, coal and salt to sugar, rum and tobacco from the West Indies, cotton from the US and India and fish from Newfoundland.

However, until the beginning of the eighteenth century Liverpool was relatively cut off from the landward side, hemmed in by marshes which were difficult to cross even in good weather. This hampered trade, and there was a significant push towards improvements in canal, road and rail transport. The first industrial turnpike in Lancashire was opened in 1727 between Liverpool and Prescot, and was soon extended to link up with the rest of the industrial northwest.

The coming of the railway in the early nineteenth century solved the problem of the slow movement of cotton between Liverpool and Manchester, the major textiles centre of the UK; it was said that before the two cities were linked by rail, bales of cotton often sat on the Liverpool dockside for weeks, taking longer to reach Manchester from Liverpool than they had taken to reach Liverpool from the US. When the railway was opened in 1830 half a million people turned up to line the route between Liverpool and Manchester, watching Stevenson's Rocket along with seven other locomotives as they made the first of what would be many journeys along this historic line.

URBAN ARCHITECTURE

The architecture of Liverpool reflects its history as a rapidly growing mercantile centre. The march of progress has driven repeated cycles of redevelopment around the port, and virtually nothing remains of the original medieval settlement; the oldest surviving city-centre building dates back only as far as the early eighteenth century, although Croxteth Hall and Speke Hall, both originally outside the city, were built in the sixteenth century.

Many of Liverpool's best and most impressive buildings were erected as headquarters for trading organisations, shipping firms and insurance companies. Others were built as civic buildings for the city's administrators, and of course the Victorian system of interconnected docks is central

GETTYIMAGES

to Liverpool's history. The city's two cathedrals, both built in the twentieth century, are appropriately connected by Hope Street, and development continues with the Mann Island Buildings and the planned Liverpool Waters skyscraper scheme.

The city's famous waterside vista is formed by the Three Graces of the Pier Head – the Royal Liver Building crowned by the famous Liver Birds, the Cunard Building and the Port of Liverpool Building. The Liver Birds are the symbol of Liverpool and are thought to derive from the eagles on the crest of King John who founded the city by Royal Charter in 1207, but the common wisdom these days is that the birds are cormorants with a sprig of laver (seaweed) in their beaks. Whatever their species, they have looked down on the Mersey for over a century, representing the first sight of Liverpool for incoming ships and settlers, and the last sight of the city for those departing in the hope of better lives abroad.

THE MERSEY FERRIES

The Mersey ferry fleet operates across the Mersey between Liverpool and the Wirral, providing a vital communication and trading link which has been in operation at least since the twelfth century. The first record of a ferry service dates from 1150, when Benedictine monks from the priory at Birkenhead would charge a small fare to row passengers across the river (then considerably wider than it is now).

The number of ferry licences and crossing points grew down the years, although the boats remained at the mercy of the weather, with the Mersey's famously thick fogs often putting a literal stop to the crossings for days on end. Steam ferries were introduced in 1815, and the crossings came under municipal ownership in the mid-nineteenth century. Two Mersey steamers, the Iris and the Daffodil, saw action in the First World War, being pressed into service as troop ships during naval raids in Belgium. Their shallow draft meant they could skim over the top of naval mines, and both vessels were damaged by enemy fire during different engagements. They received a hero's welcome when they eventually arrived back in Merseyside, and were renamed the Royal Iris and the Royal Daffodil in recognition of their service – names which have travelled down the years with different vessels. The current fleet consists of the Royal Daffodil, the Royal Iris of the Mersey and the Snowdrop. Under different names and during many refits these three vessels have served the river for over fifty years, and two of them continue to do so despite competition from the road tunnels and rail links across the river.

MERSEYBEAT

Of course, no book on Liverpool would be complete without a mention of the city's most famous recent export – the Merseybeat music genre. The movement exploded out of Liverpool

in the late 1950s, with the city's urban deprivation, industrial decline and social solidarity combining with the thriving Irish immigrant population to produce bands such as Gerry and the Pacemakers, the Dakotas and the Searchers. They were born out of the declining skiffle scene, and were also heavily influenced by the US rock and roll, rhythm and soul of the 1950s.

Although there were many other bands in Liverpool around this time (some estimate around 350 groups playing pubs, clubs and dance halls during the early 1960s), Merseybeat's best-known and most successful exponents were undoubtedly the Beatles. The band was formed by John Lennon in 1957 while he was still a student at Quarry Bank School (now Calderstones School), and the group, made up at various times of Lennon, Paul McCartney, George Harrison, Ringo Starr, Stuart Sutcliffe and Pete Best, built their reputation during the early 1960s playing clubs in Hamburg and the famous Cavern Club in Mathew Street.

Beatlemania took firm hold in 1963, sweeping the Fab Four (John, Paul, George and Ringo) to global fame under the guidance of Brian Epstein and George Martin. A string of hit albums and singles followed, with the boys conquering America and the rest of the world until their acrimonious split in 1970. They carried on working independently and sometimes together, continuing to contribute to the legacy of one of the most influential movements British pop music has ever seen.

HILLSBOROUGH

The Hillsborough disaster, which occurred on 15 April 1989, remains one of the greatest tragedies ever to hit British football. Shortly after kick-off in an FA cup semi-final match between Liverpool and Nottingham Forest, ninety-six Liverpool fans were crushed to death in the Leppings Lane stand at Hillsborough stadium in Sheffield when police allowed supporters to pour into already overcrowded pens.

Some fans managed to climb side fences to escape or were hauled to safety by fellow supporters in the stands above, but many were caught in a human press when a crush barrier broke and fans began to fall on top of each other. The game was stopped after six minutes, fans tore down advertising hoardings to use as stretchers and the emergency services arrived on the scene, but it was too late for ninety-six people, many of whom might have survived if medical treatment had been offered promptly.

The 1990 Taylor Report into the disaster led to the elimination of standing terraces at major football stadiums in England, Wales and Scotland, and an independent panel in 2012 concluded that Liverpool fans were in no way to blame for the disaster; in fact it was caused by the failure of police control, which was then covered up by the alteration of statements and other actions. The Prime Minister, South Yorkshire Police, the FA and The Sun newspaper all issued apologies for their organisations' respective roles in the disaster.

The Hillsborough ninety-six will never be forgotten at Anfield, across Merseyside and throughout the world, with many clubs and supporters touched by the disaster and continuing to honour the victims. They, and Liverpool FC, will never walk alone.

FAMOUS LOCALS

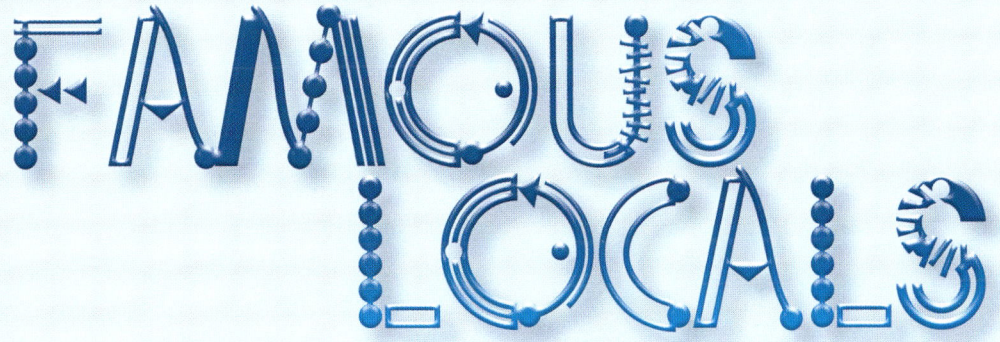

Apart from the Beatles and Wayne Rooney, Liverpool has produced a huge number of famous people. The city has been home to politicians, musicians, artists, sportsmen, writers and scientists of all generations, and continues to produce some of the country's most important and influential people.

JEREMIAH HORROCKS/CREATIVE COMMONS

JEREMIAH HORROCKS was born in Toxteth in 1618, the son of a watchmaker. He went up to Cambridge to read Divinity aged 14, but he had no interest in taking religious orders and returned to Liverpool three years later without graduating. His passion was astrology; he was self-taught and self-funded, buying the best telescope he could afford and making his own instruments with the help of his father and uncles. He was the first to prove that the moon followed an elliptical orbit around the Earth and he also correctly predicted a transit of

Venus, using his observations to make a well-informed guess about the size of the planet. Tragically he died suddenly aged only 22 and many of his papers were lost during the Civil War and the Great Fire of London, but among his fellow astronomers he is deservedly known as the father of English astronomy.

JOSEPH WILLIAMSON

was a businessman, philanthropist and eccentric. Born in 1769 the son of a Barnsley glassblower, he made his fortune in Liverpool buying and selling tobacco, and then embarked on an idiosyncratic career of seemingly useless philanthropy. He employed men to move large quantities of materials from one place to another and then back again, and supervised the excavation of an extensive system of tunnels and underground halls in the Edge Hill area (earning him the nickname of the Mole of Edge Hill).

His motives have been questioned down the years, with some suggesting that the tunnels were built to provide a refuge against an apocalypse which Williamson believed was coming, but the most likely explanation is that he was simply doing what he could to alleviate unemployment, giving men a weekly wage for honest (if pointless) labour without demeaning them with offers of charity.

WILLIAM GLADSTONE

was born in a house on Rodney Street in 1809, the son of a Scottish merchant family. He went on to become a Liberal politician who served as Prime Minister four times between 1868 and 1894; he remains the oldest person to hold the post of PM, resigning for the last time at the age of 84. Throughout his political career he was concerned with removing economic restraints, reducing taxation and enhancing trade. He was a great orator and was known for his liberalism, his rivalry with Benjamin Disraeli and his poor relationship with Queen Victoria, who once remarked, "He always addresses me as if I were a public meeting." It is a little-known fact that for leisure and recreation Gladstone was an enthusiastic tree-feller, finding exercise as well as relaxation by wielding an axe. However, he always replaced the trees he felled with new saplings.

ELEANOR RATHBONE,

born in 1872, was the daughter of the social reformer William Rathbone, and she began her career working alongside her father to investigate and improve social and industrial conditions in Liverpool. She was an independent member of Liverpool City Council for twenty-five years and entered parliament in 1929, concentrating on women's issues and arguing for a system of family allowances paid directly to mothers. She championed women's suffrage and their rights to economic independence, and saw the Family Allowances Act pass into law a year before her death in 1946. The School of Law and Social Justice at the University of Liverpool bears her name.

KEN DODD/CREATIVE COMMONS

KEN DODD

was born in the Knotty Ash area of Liverpool in 1927, and over sixty years in show business he has remained one of the city's best-loved stand-up comedians. His frizzy hair and buck teeth (the result of a childhood cycling accident), his trademark greeting of "How tickled I am!" and his rapid-fire one-liners have won him huge audiences and made him a household name. Despite his age he is still renowned for his long performances; indeed, he once held the record for the longest joke-telling session, telling 1500 jokes in three-and-a-half hours. His stage act usually features his tickling stick and the Diddy Men, who work in the Jam Butty Mines in Dodd's native Knotty Ash.

CARLA LANE

is one of Liverpool's best loved writers and dramatists. Born Romana Barrack in 1937, she is the creator of some of the city's most popular depictions in modern culture – in particular, The Liver Birds, a sitcom set in 1970s Merseyside and starring Nerys Hughes and Polly James, and Bread, the story of the ne'er-do-well

CILLA BLACK,

born Priscilla White in 1943, is a singer, actress and entertainer. She was determined to break into show business from an early age, taking a job as cloakroom attendant at the Cavern Club and impressing the Beatles with her singing talents. She

Boswell family from the inner-city Dingle area. Early in her career she collaborated with Myra Talyor, with the two meeting at the Adelphi Hotel to write. More recently she has been known for her animal rights activism and for returning her OBE in protest against the award of a CBE to the managing director of a company practising animal experimentation.

ALISON STEADMAN/CREATIVE COMMONS

ALISON STEADMAN

is one of the greats of British theatre. She was born on Merseyside in 1946 and went to school in Childwall before going to drama school and meeting Mike Leigh, whom she married and with whom she has done some of her finest work.

She created the role of the monstrous Abigail in Abigail's Party, and has appeared on stage and on the big and small screens in everything from Shakespeare and Jane Austen to Fat Friends and Gavin and Stacey. She is one of Britain's best-loved character actresses, with an instantly recognisable voice and a talent for mimicry and characterisation. was introduced to Brian Epstein by John Lennon, and her early career was characterised by collaborations with various members of the Beatles. She branched out into television, presenting her own series and acting in sitcoms before presenting *Blind Date* and *Surprise Surprise*. She continues to work in show business, guest-presenting on shows such as Loose Women and The Paul O'Grady Show (another proud Scouser), and appearing as herself in shows from Coronation Street to Benidorm.